Today What If...

Graham Hodgson

Bloomington, IN  Milton Keynes, UK

author HOUSE™

AuthorHouse™
1663 Liberty Drive, Suite 200
Bloomington, IN 47403
www.authorhouse.com
Phone: 1-800-839-8640

AuthorHouse™ UK Ltd.
500 Avebury Boulevard
Central Milton Keynes, MK9 2BE
www.authorhouse.co.uk
Phone: 08001974150

First published by AuthorHouse 7/13/2006

ISBN: 1-4259-2324-0 (sc)

Printed in the United States of America
Bloomington, Indiana

This book is printed on acid-free paper.

Introduction

My name is Graham Hodgson and I am 45 years old. I will now give you a script of how I would like my life to be in the present:

With a loving wife, sharing and being
there for one another.

Children to encourage and to experience
the special bond only that relationship can bring.

A big house by the sea filled
with friends coming to enjoy.

Money in the bank,
for the security that it brings.

Now I will tell you how it actually is:

I am single with a growing list
of failed relationships.

I do not have any children of my own.

I live in a room at my friends' house.

I am a recently discharged bankrupt
with no money in the bank!

In case you are now thinking that I have told you this in order to feel sorry for me, this could not be further from the truth. This discrepancy between what I want and what I actually have has been a blessing for it has led me to question how this has come about.

I question whether the circumstances that I am in are totally out of my control and the product of a mixture of bad luck or timing, whatever. Or is there one constant throughout all of them that I do have control over. The answer to that is yes – myself!

All of the circumstances that I now face are there because of MY responses, actions, desires, beliefs – I am totally responsible for my life.

For me this is a groundbreaking discovery, how many of us want to take full responsibility for how we are?

Now that I have linked my circumstances to my own desires, actions etc…It is easy to see how I can change what is in front of me – by CHOOSING the thoughts, responses, actions to suit the picture of myself that I desire.

I know that this requires continuous vigilance but I have total faith that I am more than able to do this – because that is what I am INSTRUCTING the mind. Anyone for a trip to the seaside?

TODAY WHAT IF...

Everybody in the world smiled at just one more person.

That would be 6 billion more smiles each and every day, do you think that would make the world a brighter place?!

Now what about another two smiles...

TODAY WHAT IF...

The situation I was in is totally my own doing and was there because I have made it that way.

Would I choose to change anything so that my situation was more prosperous, happy, healthy etc...

TODAY WHAT IF...

I saved just one pound towards those Christmas presents, holidays, whatever.

Each year I would have an extra £365.

Now what if I were to save £2...

TODAY WHAT IF...

Aliens attacked the world.

Do you think that we all might pull together and forget our differences as in the case of the tsunami?

Now what if we do not wait until aliens attack the world...

TODAY WHAT IF...

I thought that whatever project I undertook I could not fail to complete.

What sort of projects would I be thinking of?

If I really could not fail wouldn't I reach for the heavens?

TODAY WHAT IF...

I watched half an hours less television and gave the attention to the family, exercise, special project or whatever.

That would be an extra week per year.

Now what if I were to watch one hour less...

TODAY WHAT IF...

I woke up half an hour earlier than normal.

If I done this every day, that would be an extra week per year awake.

If I earn £200 per week then there is the chance to enjoy a few more little luxuries...

TODAY WHAT IF...

I looked upon my work as a return of service for the gifts that I have received.

Would this help me to view my occupation in a different way?

TODAY WHAT IF...

I viewed the bills that I get as invoices for goods received.

Would I see them in a different way?

TODAY WHAT IF...

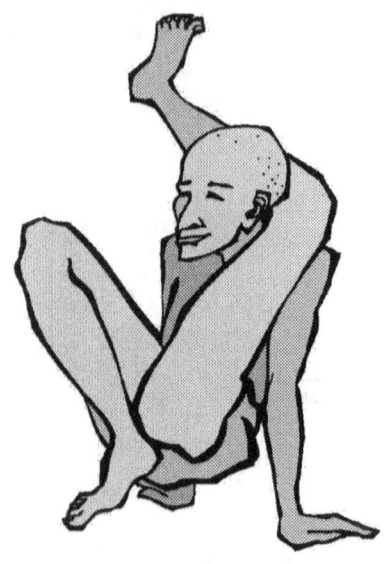

I contemplated my body as something miraculous that no amount of money, any scientist or philosopher can even get near to explaining.

Would I take care of it in a different way?

TODAY WHAT IF...

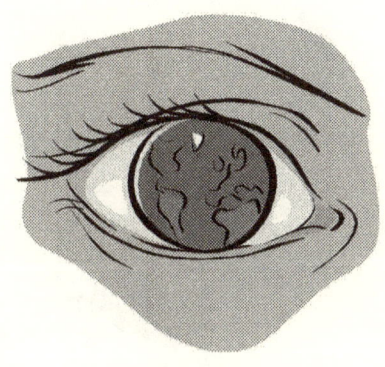

I was to view the world as a spectator rather than someone to whom everything happens.

Would I still feel the same intensity about what was going on?

TODAY WHAT IF...

I considered myself
extremely privileged to be
born a human being, with
the opportunities that come
because of the special
abilities that we have.

TODAY WHAT IF...

I looked upon problems as challenges that I am more than able to meet if I apply myself to them.

TODAY WHAT IF...

I chose to change negative thoughts that enter my head into positive ones that lift my spirits.

Would I then be better company?

TODAY WHAT IF...

I woke up and felt fully in charge of my destiny, full of energy to meet the day's demands.

Would I feel more empowered?

TODAY WHAT IF...

I knew that the thoughts that circulate in my head, if mixed with emotion, would one day be the physical circumstances that I am faced with.

What thoughts would I choose to dwell on?

TODAY WHAT IF...

The old saying that what goes around comes around is true.

What would I choose to go with in order to receive back?

TODAY WHAT IF...

I view my emotions and check
to see if they are being used
to work for my highest good,
knowing that I have full
control over them.

TODAY WHAT IF...

My thoughts were not governed by the actions of others but by what I choose to think and believe.

Would this change my habitual responses in any way?

Today What if...

It is true that where there is a WILL there is a WAY – what is it that I WILL so that the way will become available?

TODAY WHAT IF...

The whole world really is just
a stage – what magnificent
part do I want to play?

TODAY WHAT IF...

I took a different route to work and engaged my colleagues in a different way.

Would this help me to look at things afresh?

TODAY WHAT IF...

I walked an extra mile.

If I done that everyday it would be 365 miles more per year, using up over 30,000 calories or 3,333 grams of fat!

Now what about 1.5 miles...

TODAY WHAT IF...

There was to be a channel on television devoted entirely to good news.

Would this help me to see that perhaps the world is not all bad...

TODAY WHAT IF...

I truly believed that I had an inner voice that was completely able to guide me to all the best decisions for my welfare.

Would I spend more time trying to cultivate and listen to this voice rather than rely on advice from numerous different sources?

TODAY WHAT IF...

When I sat down for breakfast cereal I considered the work gone into what is front of me.

Farmers to sow the seeds, labourers to reap the harvest, warehouse workers, transport workers, factory workers, management, sales, retail...perhaps I might look on it with a little more gratitude.

TODAY WHAT IF...

I got curious about something, maybe how the television works or how Blair became Prime Minister!

Would I start to question things a bit more and find life a bit more interesting?

TODAY WHAT IF...

At the end of the day I was to reflect on my actions throughout it; is there anything I would have done different, what were the highlights etc...

Then let them go with the knowledge that tomorrow I have the chance to improve, enjoy, learn...

TODAY WHAT IF...

There is something that I really desire, I find someone who has already acquired it, whether it be a skill or possession, then try to gain advice about how they achieved it in order for me to follow – no point in re-inventing the wheel!

TODAY WHAT IF...

Everyone in the world was to choose one person and do something special for him or her, even if just a kind word.

Would 6 billion more good deeds make the world a little better place?

TODAY WHAT IF...

Everyone in the world was to forgive one action or word received from another.

Perhaps 6 billion acts of forgiveness might trigger off an era of peace.

TODAY WHAT IF...

Everyone in Europe put £1
in to a great big pot, then
the proceeds were used for
famine relief or some worthy
project - £250,000,000
would go a long way.

TODAY WHAT IF...

I accepted the mind as being like
a giant compact storage disc with
myself as a playback machine.

If I access the right area
all the information I need
is there to make available
for my use.

TODAY WHAT IF...

I decided to ask for something I wanted, even if it is just a helping hand.

Would this open up a channel for me to be able to receive more?

TODAY WHAT IF...

I examined the beliefs that have led me to where I am.

Are they still benefiting me or could I replace any of them to improve on today's situation?

TODAY WHAT IF...

I labelled everyone I met with the term, brother/sister/mother/ father, etc...

Would this enable me to view them in a more kindly way?

TODAY WHAT IF...

I believed everyone loved me.

Would there be any better feeling?

TODAY WHAT IF...

I paid full attention to what is in front of me and had confidence that, in that moment, I was fully able to meet whatever demands there were.

Would I accomplish more?

TODAY WHAT IF...

I wrote myself a goal that I wished to accomplish and immediately started to plan a way of attaining it.

Might this help towards clarifying what it is that I desire?

TODAY WHAT IF...

I believed that, instead of being separate to everyone and everything else, somehow I was miraculously linked to them - a part which is essential to the well being of the whole and totally unable to be parted from it.

Would I then ever need to feel lonely or of no use?

TODAY WHAT IF...

At the end of the evening I planned some details for the next day.

Would this help to structure my time to be used more efficiently?

TODAY WHAT IF...

I spent 5 minutes contemplating something beautiful like a picture of a sunset, a lit candle etc...Would this help me to touch a deeper aspect of myself that is not affected by the worries of the day?

Now what about 10 minutes...

TODAY WHAT IF...

I reviewed the goals that
I have made and checked
whether I am keeping to the
plans or that my goals are
serving the way I am today.

TODAY WHAT IF...

I considered that the limitations I see in others are the very things that are lacking in myself.

Would I have a clearer idea on where to look in order to try and improve?

TODAY WHAT IF...

I was to dwell in all my senses.

I really tasted my food.

I took a good look at all the beauty that surrounds me.

I felt the textures of my clothes.

I listened intently to all the variety of sounds.

I smelt all the differences in the aromas around me.

Would I feel more in touch with what is going on?

TODAY WHAT IF...

I viewed each and every minute of the day as exclusively mine to do with whatever pleases me?

What do I want my moments to say about my pleasures?

TODAY WHAT IF...

I looked upon each moment as being now – no yesterday, tomorrow or any other time.

If I am always alive in the moment now, would that not make me eternal?

If this is the case, is there any moment that I need to worry?

TODAY WHAT IF...

I died?

Would all my friends stop being able
to enjoy life?
Would absolutely no one else be able
to do my work?
Would the economy crash?

**If these things
don't happen then
maybe I could see my
responsibilities in a
different light?**

TODAY WHAT IF...

I took account of my finances to see
if there is any way I can improve
them.

Is my money making
money – if not then could
I move some to an account
that does?
Could I move my debts to
somewhere that charges
less interest?

TODAY WHAT IF...

I was to view every single thing in the Universe as a ball of energy, including myself.

What if this energy can be transformed into just about anything, would this open up possibilities?

TODAY WHAT IF...

I looked at my reflection in the mirror and totally accepted myself for how I looked and how I was in that moment.

Would this stop some of the self-recriminations?

TODAY WHAT IF...

I sang a joyous song in my heart in thanks for being alive!

TODAY WHAT IF...

I did something frivolous to remind myself of the freedom of being like a child.

Would this lift my spirits?

TODAY WHAT IF...

I viewed myself as being made of rubber.

This way I could meet any demands of the day in a flexible manner and be able to accommodate them more than in a rigid approach.

TODAY WHAT IF...

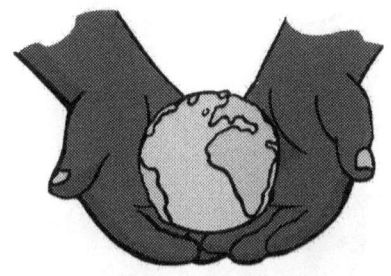

I saw love as being inclusive instead of exclusive.

In other words if I was to view all people alike and try to find the common bond between us – even if it is just that we are all human!

TODAY WHAT IF...

I thought to myself 'can I be that which I observe?'

As I observe everything (including the body and mind) then I must wonder if my true identity is attached to any of it.

Would this help me to be a little freer?

TODAY WHAT IF...

I looked at the mind as just that
– mind – and not attach my sense of
ownership to it.

Would this free me
from limiting ideas about
myself?

TODAY WHAT IF...

I thought of the body as an instrument for my use instead of being the totality of myself.

Would I use it in any different way?

TODAY WHAT IF...

I viewed the company that I kept, the books I read, music I listened to and television I watched, as food for the mind.

Would I choose to nourish it in any other way to keep it healthy?

TODAY WHAT IF...

I believed that the world is full of all the things that I desire and I can have them all as long as I do not lay claim to them.

Would I still hang on so dearly to the things I have accumulated so far?

TODAY WHAT IF...

I believed that everyone was born equal and that the only true responsibility I have is to myself.

Would I be able to conduct myself so as to be an example for others to follow?

TODAY WHAT IF...

My mind was like a gun, thoughts like the loaded gun and spoken words like the fired bullets.

All the time the thoughts are contained within the mind they can be withheld from any reaction but once they leave as words there is no turning back.

TODAY WHAT IF...

I was to view each moment as being now and I gave it to who or whatever was in front of me.

Could anyone ever give anymore?

Today What if...

Each moment was one of pure creation with which I was able to create whatever dreams I have.

What would be the dreams my moments created – would I go for the big fish?

TODAY WHAT IF...

Everyone was so grateful for the kindness of others that they passed it on to someone else.

Would this not ensure that only one act of kindness would wrap completely around the world?

TODAY WHAT IF...

I considered how
many worries, cares,
responsibilities etc...I had
when I was fast asleep?

Miraculously they seem to disappear,
just to resurface when I am awake
-was I a different person when
asleep?

Perhaps I could bring a
little of my 'carefree'
attitude into my daytime?

Today What if...

There was something I felt strongly about that I wrote a letter to my MP or rallied for the cause.

Would this help to stir up a little apathy?

TODAY WHAT IF...

It was true that love is all around but only if I CHOSE to see it.

Would I try to open my eyes a little more?

TODAY WHAT IF...

Happiness is in always in the moment now.

Do I have to wait for some circumstance or another before I become happy?

TODAY WHAT IF...

I imagined my dreams coming true in vivid detail.

Would this help me remain focussed on what it is I want?

TODAY WHAT IF...

I decided that it was my birthright to be happy, healthy and wealthy.

Would I make a claim for each?

TODAY WHAT IF...

I imagined my heart to be a well full
of a loving stream.

How often would I be
taking a drink?

TODAY WHAT IF...

There was something that the world
needs that only I can do.

How important would this
make me feel?

TODAY WHAT IF...

All my actions are unique and leave a lasting impression on the world around me.

What impressions would I choose to leave?

TODAY WHAT IF...

I gave power to the importance of my desires as a way of living a life of creativity.

TODAY WHAT IF...

I considered meditation as a way of releasing my habitual thought patterns that I follow throughout the day.

Perhaps this would enable a little time to recoup some energy that could be used for something that pleases me – or others!

TODAY WHAT IF...

I was to believe that the best thing I can do for the poor is not to be one of them.

How would I manifest prosperity in my life now?

TODAY WHAT IF...

Focus of attention was like the match
that starts the fire - it has to be
struck at the object and then the
desired effect will take place.

Would I want to focus more for my desires to take place?

TODAY WHAT IF...

I was convinced that where I am today is in no way an indication to where I can be in the future – just think of J.K.Rowling!

Would this help me to concentrate more on where I do want to be?

TODAY WHAT IF...

All my past actions were necessary stepping-stones in order for me to reach my enlightening future.

Would I view them in a different light?

TODAY WHAT IF...

I made a decision to be better than yesterday.

To look for some improvement, no matter how small, in order to keep things on the up!

Today What if...

I considered myself as on a stationery train and the world as one on the other track. When another train goes by it appears that I am the one moving, however I know that is not true.

Perhaps it is everything else that moves and I am always just still to enjoy the show.

TODAY WHAT IF...

I realised the importance of consistent action in order to bring my ambitions to life.

What actions would I take today in order to make my dreams come true?

TODAY WHAT IF...

I was to keep a very close eye for any opportunities that come my way.

If I viewed things in a slightly different way, could today be the one where my true vocation appeared?

TODAY WHAT IF...

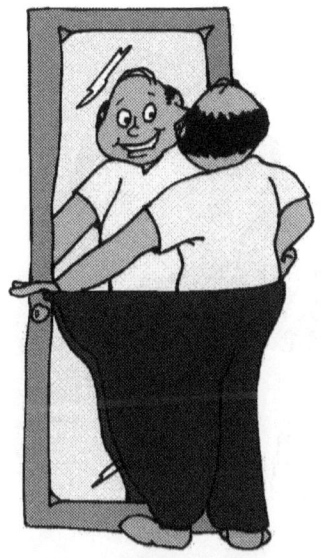

I reflected that even the body that I have now was completely different 3 months ago.

Everything is constantly changing.

What if I were to embrace change instead of resisting or fighting against it, would this help to make life less of a battle?

TODAY WHAT IF...

I took Shakespeare's advice to adopt a virtue if I do not already possess it.

Which virtue would I like to try out in order to establish as part of my personality?

TODAY WHAT IF...

I could see all the words that I spoke during the day and the effects they had.

Would I be using the same words tomorrow?

TODAY WHAT IF...

I was able to weigh my actions on a set of scales – positive one side, negative the other.

Would I need to change any in order to tip the balance on the side I want?

Today What if...

I took just one action to make my environment better, maybe some fresh flowers, a tidy up or I told someone how much I like them.

Would this make the day just a little more appealing?

TODAY WHAT IF...

I decided that I could spend my time
DESIGNING a GRAND LIFE rather
than just planning to get by.

Would I design it as it is
now or are there major
new blueprints needed for
success?

TODAY WHAT IF...

Even with action, I need to PERSIST
with my goals in order to establish a
link to them.

Would I need to look again at how many actions I am still taking?

TODAY WHAT IF...

To give really is better than to receive.

What is that I can give that will make life just that little bit grander?

TODAY WHAT IF...

It was great to get passionate about something in life, to look for something that I could really get into.

This maybe a hobby, a person, work or anything.

If I done this would I find life more interesting?

TODAY WHAT IF...

Nature really does abhor a vacuum – could I create any space in my life to be filled with some new things that I want now.

What about that wardrobe...

TODAY WHAT IF...

I congratulated myself on just waking up – after all it is a pretty magnificent feat!

After this I could speak encouraging words to myself about the day ahead.

Would this put me in a good frame of mind to start the day?

TODAY WHAT IF...

I selected what times I was going to devote to the most important actions and then stuck to them.

Would this help avoid things just dragging on...

TODAY WHAT IF...

I was to fill the day with faith that I could achieve the best outcomes for myself and be good company to all those I came into contact with.

Would this change the way I approached each moment?

TODAY WHAT IF...

I was to expect something nice to happen but be completely unaffected if it doesn't.

Would the air of expectancy add an excitement to the day that might not otherwise be there?

TODAY WHAT IF...

I asked myself the question 'did I
wake up as myself'?

If I answer 'yes' then
exactly whom do I have to
answer to throughout the
day for any problems, for
any actions that I take or
circumstances around me?

TODAY WHAT IF...

All of the people in the world were the covers on the books but inside there was only ONE story.

Would this help me to look further than just the cover?

TODAY WHAT IF...

I was to reflect that all movement comes from stillness and all sound comes from silence.

Therefore the source of everything, including myself, is still and silent – or at peace – always.

TODAY WHAT IF...

(enter your own here!)

Recommendations

There are numerous books/authors that I could recommend here but I feel one of the best ways of finding the book you want is to just walk in and buy one — let your instinct be your guide!

However I do have a list of websites that I feel have helped myself enormously in my search for greater meaning as follows:

www.free-positive-thought.com

www.choosetoprosper.com

www.scienceofgettingrich.net

I haven't actually used this one but I thought it might well be useful for beginners —

www.meditationcenter.com

Then of course there is my own www.todaywhatif.com

www.ingramcontent.com/pod-product-compliance
Lightning Source LLC
Chambersburg PA
CBHW020309290526
45784CB00003B/1437